Title Insurance Tips and Secrets™

Published By:

Distressed Real Estate Institute, LLC.
7040 West Palmetto Park Road, Suite 4-675
Boca Raton Florida 33433
Telephone: (800) 617-2884

ISBN: 978-0-9843417-0-2
Library of Congress Control Number: 2009943338

Title Insurance Tips and Secrets™

Kevin S. Tacher

and

Lex Levinrad

About the Author

Kevin S. Tacher – Kevin grew up on Long Island, NY. Prior to moving to Florida in 2001 Kevin was a fire fighter and Fire Safety Director for the Crowne Plaza Hotel in NYC. He moved to Florida just twenty days prior to September 11th. Upon arriving in Florida, Kevin began working for a mortgage lender and then eventually earned his licenses as a mortgage consultant, real estate broker and title agent. Armed with the extensive knowledge and experience of the real estate industry, in 2003 Kevin opened his own business Independence Title. Kevin's experience gave him the ability to provide the full range of services for homeowners and real estate investors throughout the State of Florida. Kevin is a Director with Business Network International (BNI) and a Certified Endless Referrals Consultant with Burg International, which enables him to further fulfill his passion of providing others with valuable connections and resources to ensure their success.

As a published author and national public speaker Kevin has shared the stage with some of the best motivational and real estate speakers in the country.

For more information about Kevin please visit www.KevinTacher.com or www.MyTitleCo.com or call (954) 335-9305.

About the Author

Lex Levinrad - Lex has been a full time distressed real estate investor since 2003. He has been involved in buying, rehabbing, wholesaling, renting, and selling hundreds of houses in South Florida. Lex is the founder and CEO of the Distressed Real Estate Institute, which trains beginning distressed real estate investors about how to find wholesale real estate deals. Lex specializes in buying foreclosures, short sales and bank owned properties. The Distressed Real Estate Institute offers home study courses, boot camps, and private mentoring for real estate investors. Lex has authored many books about investing in real estate and is an accomplished national speaker who has shared the stage with some of the countries best real estate speakers. Lex is also the founder of the Distressed Real Estate Investors Association and co-founder of the Port St Lucie Real Estate Investors Association. For more information about Lex please visit www.LexLevinrad.com or call (800) 617-2884.

Dedication

To my daughter Lindsay Rose who continues to be the inspiration in my life.

To my co-author Lex Levinrad who has been right by my side throughout the roller coaster we experienced in the real estate business over the past several years. Thank you for your guidance, support, mentoring and most of all your friendship.

To my dear friend Cynthia Benchick, if it wasn't for you I would not be where I am today. Your support and encouragement is exceptional and I am honored to be a part of your world class team of real estate professionals.

Introduction to Title Insurance

Before we get into the details of title insurance, I would like to introduce you to the history and background of what title insurance is.

Title insurance is issued in the United States upon the purchase of real property. Issuance of a title insurance policy ensures that you have clear and marketable title to a property when you purchase it. Title insurance has many facets to it like lien searches, title commitments, title policies etc. which we will be discussing in further detail throughout this book. Wikipedia defines title insurance as "indemnity insurance against financial loss from defects in title to real property and from the invalidity or unenforceability of mortgage liens".

Title Insurance is unique to the U.S and is not offered in many other countries. The need for title insurance came about due to the deficiency of the U.S land record laws which did not protect a purchaser of real property form title defects in the past. Title insurance does not insure the future of the title only the past. The purpose of title insurance is to protect a buyer of a property and ensure that prior to purchasing that property, all outstanding liens, judgments etc. that are attached to that property are satisfied or resolved. Once resolved, the title will be considered clear and marketable, meaning the property can be sold. The title company then issues a title policy which outlines specifically the amount of title insurance the policy covers (usually the purchase price or the amount of the loan recorded against the property). It is possible to buy real estate without a title policy, but to do so would be extremely foolish since it would expose the buyer to any problems that occurred with that property prior to them purchasing it.

Title insurance protects the owner of the property as well as the lender's financial interest in the real property against loss due to defects in title, liens, judgments, unrecorded liens, code enforcement violations, city liens, unpaid water bills, etc. A lien that shows up in a title search will cause the title to be clouded (defective title) and will make the title unmarketable. What this means is that unless the buyer is willing to buy the property with the existing defect, the property cannot be conveyed, sold or transferred prior to this defect being resolved.

Title insurance also will defend against a lawsuit attacking the title because the title policy covers the insured and will reimburse the insured for the actual monetary loss incurred, up to the dollar amount of insurance provided by the policy. It is important to remember that title insurance protects the owner and/or lender from defects that arose prior to the date of purchase. It is not like traditional insurance that protects you forward.

Components of Title Insurance

When you are working with a title company or attorney for your closing there are many issues that are related to the settlement of your purchase or sale of residential property. The following are the main items:

- Title Insurance
- Title Policy
- Title Commitment
- Title Search
- Title Examination
- Lien Search
- Closing Costs
- Settlement Statement (HUD - 1)
- Inspection
- Property Taxes
- Survey
- Casualty and Flood Insurance
- Mortgages

The first item (title insurance) was covered in the introduction. Title insurance is the amount of insurance that you have covering your real estate transaction (usually the amount of the purchase price). The policy that is issued by the insurance company indicating what is covered and what is not covered, is known as a title policy. Before you can get a title policy you will need a title commitment. The title commitment is issued before the closing and tells you what will and will not be covered. The final title policy is issued at closing and is based on the information in the title commitment.

Title Commitment

The title commitment reflects who currently owns the property, legal description, along with the parcel identification number of the property. This is also known as a land description. This information is located on Schedule A of the title commitment. Schedule A shows who the owner of record is, the buyer, the purchase price, the lender and the loan amount.

Schedule B of the title commitment is sub divided into Schedule B-I and Schedule B-II. Schedule B-I shows **requirements** that are necessary in order to close and issue the title insurance policy. Schedule B-II shows **exceptions** which are items that the title policy will not cover and which are excluded and not covered by the title insurance policy.

Schedule B-I is the requirements page which lists the documents that must be produced and/or signed as well as any items that need to be satisfied prior to closing. This is required at closing for the title to be transferred from the seller to the buyer. Schedule B-I also lists all liens such as mortgages, property taxes, judgments, code enforcement violations etc. which must be released and satisfied at or prior to closing.

By issuing a title commitment, the underwriter is committing to issuing a title policy to the buyer, provided that the requirements of the title commitment are satisfied prior to closing. For this reason, you should always request a copy and review your title commitment prior to closing. As a title agent, I am amazed at how few buyers request to read their title commitment. You should review the title commitment, and if you don't know how to read it then you should have your Title Company or attorney review it and explain it to you.

The information on the title commitment is the result of information which shows up on the title search. The title search searches public record to find out who owns the property and also searches public records for all liens, judgments and claims of liens etc. You should always have your title company perform a title search. If you are getting a title policy and title insurance (and you should always get this) then the title policy and the title commitment will be automatically included.

Some wholesale real estate investors try and save money by not getting title insurance. This is a big mistake. You should always get title insurance, even if you are doing a simultaneous or double closing since you want the end buyer to be protected as much as the first buyer on the first transaction. Regardless of whether you are the buyer or the seller on either closing you will still be held responsible if there is a problem with the chain of title. Saving a little money on title insurance now could cost you thousands in the long run. Do not skip this step regardless of what others tell you.

Schedule B-II lists the exceptions. This is the most important part of your title commitment and should be reviewed very carefully by you if you are the buyer. The reason that Schedule B-II is so important is because everything that is not covered by your title policy will be listed here. Or expressed another way, every thing that could be wrong with this property will be listed here. If you are not sure what something is you should ask your title company to explain it to you. Remember, that you are responsible for what you sign. So if you don't understand something please consult with someone that does in order for them to explain it to you in a way that you can understand.

Most properties have exceptions listed on Schedule B-II of the title commitment. Having exceptions listed is not a problem, but you should make sure that you know what they are. Some properties even have use restrictions specifying what you can and cannot do with your property.

Ultimately it is the responsibility of the seller to cure these title defects and to deliver clear and marketable title to the buyer. It is the responsibility of the buyer to read their title commitment and ask questions about all requirements and exceptions prior to closing. Do not sign until you are convinced that all requirements have been satisfied. If you are unsure consult with the title company. Be especially cautious of title companies that work for the bank. These title companies might be more interested in their relationship with the bank rather than the relationship with you. These title companies are not looking out for your best interests and do not have a relationship with you.

Marked Up Title Commitment

If you look at your title commitment carefully you will notice that there are items that are circled and/or checked off. This is known as a marked up title commitment and is very important to review. You should always ask for, and obtain, a marked up title commitment. When a company marks up a title

6

commitment, this is showing that all of the requirements listed on Schedule B-I of the title commitment for closing have been completed. In the 8 years I have been in the title insurance business this is one item that usually only experienced people ask for. As a buyer, lender, investor or real estate agent you want to make sure that the requirements have been completed. Each item that is listed on Schedule B-I should be checked off indicating that the title company has reviewed and satisfied each requirement. Ask the title company about each requirement and make sure that it is checked off and satisfied. Then ask them for a marked up title commitment. This is your written proof that the title company has satisfied these items. Only experienced real estate professionals ask for a marked up title commitment. You should always ask for a marked up title commitment. Remember that **you** are responsible for what you sign. If you don't know how to read the title commitment, then you should have your title company or attorney explain it to you. Make sure that the title company is working for you and not for someone else (like the seller, bank, real estate agent or mortgage broker etc.). This is one of the main reasons why we always tell our investors to choose their own title company. If you control where the closing takes place then you are able to guide the closing to your title company whom will look out for your best interests. Let the title company know that you want them to review the title commitment and the lien search. If you have repeat closings with a title company and establish a relationship, then you will be rewarded with world class service.

Please remember that the title commitment is a promise to insure title to your property subject to certain exceptions which are outlined in Schedule B-II. Do not forget to review the exceptions in order to have the title company or attorney remove standard exceptions that may or may not be required to be removed or satisfied prior to closing.

A marked up title commitment is where Schedule B-I is marked satisfied which indicates that all of the requirements have been cleared. The final mark up of the title commitment indicates which items are covered and which items are excluded and is the best form of evidence of insurance from the title company.

Title Policy

The title policy is what you receive after the closing from the title company or attorney. The title policy is usually in the same package as the original recorded warranty deed. You should save your title policy along with all paperwork for the property. If there was ever a problem with the title to the property you would want to make sure that you had your title policy available. You should never throw your title policy away, even after you have sold the property. If there is ever a problem with the chain of title on this property then you will need this title policy to show that you were protected.

Another reason to save your title policy is that if you sell the property within 3 years from the date of purchase or refinance at any time then you will be eligible to receive a reissue credit which will substantially reduce your title policy premium on the new transaction.

Underwriter

The underwriter is the company that is issuing the title insurance policy. In Florida, the most common underwriters are First American Title Insurance Company, Old Republic Title and Stewart Title Guaranty Company. These companies issue a title policy indicating that if there is problem with title they will cover it as long as the problem is not listed in Schedule B-II. This is exactly why you should review Schedule B-II so thoroughly.

Title Examination

The Title Examiner will research the history of the property and compile a title research report. This process is known as a title examination. There are many varied and complex issues that may arise in a normal title examination. The title examination will trace the transfer of ownership (title) of the land going back to the first purchaser. A normal title examination researches the history of the property for a period of thirty years.

It is a relatively simple procedure to trace ownership of the property as it transferred from one owner to another. This chain of title shows the history of transfer of ownership of the property and is what a title search is all about.

Researching the title to a property is complicated because previous owners may have died leaving title to the property to their heirs as designated by a will or trust. Or the owner of a property could have filed bankruptcy and the title could have been transferred to the bankruptcy trustee. The title to the property could be in the name of a Limited Liability Company also known as an LLC, of which one of the partners may be involved in a lawsuit. There may be federal tax liens placed against an owner of the property or one of the previous owners may have been in foreclosure. Title examination is extremely important. There are many issues that can arise with title. You can buy a property without title insurance but you would be foolish to do so. A thorough title examination along with a title policy will insure that if your title is well inspected your investment is protected™.

Any unresolved issue could "cloud" the title meaning that the title is not clear and marketable which could prevent the closing from occurring. If you own the property this could prevent you from ever selling it. This is why you cannot afford to not have title insurance.

Examiner

The examiner is the individual that performs the title examination. Based on the title examination, the title commitment and title policy are issued by the title company. Any exceptions listed on Schedule B-II of the title commitment need to be reviewed and cleared by the examiner. If there is a problem with the title, the title company will contact the examiner to have them review the issue and see if they can come up with a solution to resolve the issue. If they can, then the examiner will "insure over" the issue meaning that they are prepared to insure the transaction and issue a title policy without listing the item as an exception. Good title companies have good relationships with the title examiner so that any issues that come up can immediately be resolved.

Property Survey

If you are buying, selling, planning to refinance or make improvements to your property, the lender and the building department will require that you have a Boundary Survey and an Elevation Certificate. A boundary survey shows the boundary of your property which is where your property ends and your neighbors begins.

The Boundary Survey provided by a Professional Surveyor and Cartographer (map maker) graphically shows any possible encroachments or easement violations that could prevent the owner from selling the land or making improvements to it. It is critical to know if there are concrete slabs, fences, structures including utilities within easements or built onto the adjacent property. Did you know that having a Boundary (Land) Survey and Elevation Certificate are considered improvements to the property? They are!

Elevation Certificate

The elevation certificate shows how high the lot sits relative to surrounding land. Elevation is important if you are in a flood zone since properties that are elevated will have less risk of flooding and properties that are not will have increased risk. A flood determination determines if your property sits in a flood zone. The lender will require an elevation certificate if you are in a Federal Emergency Management Agency (FEMA) flood hazard zone and will require you to purchase flood insurance to protect against the risk of flood. The elevation certificate will determine how much premium you pay for your flood insurance policy.

Lenders will require that you show proof of flood insurance prior to loaning against the property. The lender can offer you a flood insurance policy but the premium will be very high since they will assume the worst elevation. Purchasing an elevation certificate will enable you to pay less for flood insurance since the elevation certificate will indicate the relative risk of flood, to the insurance company. The elevation certificate shows how high above the pre determined base flood elevation the structure sits as well as the elevations adjacent to the building.

If you are in a flood zone purchasing an elevation certificate will save you money in premiums over the long haul.

Lien Search

The lien search is typically performed by a lien search company and is not the same as a title search. A lien search lets you know if there are any unrecorded issues pertaining to the property, which could be encumbering the property. Some of the most common unrecorded concerns are unpaid water and utility bills, code enforcement violations and open permits. Please note that unpaid electric bills follow the owner and do not attach to the property itself.

A lien is meant to protect parties that have an interest in the property. For example if you get a mortgage to buy a property then the bank wants to ensure that you cannot transfer the property to anyone else without their mortgage first being paid off or satisfied. The way that the bank does this is by recording a lien against the property. A mortgage would be recorded as a first mortgage lien. A second mortgage would be recorded as a second mortgage lien and so forth.

Liens have priority. When a property is sold the first lien is paid off first. If there is anything left over then the second lien is paid and if there is anything left, then the third lien is paid.

Liens, judgments and their priorities are a very complicated topic beyond the scope of this book. Lien law is confusing, for example property taxes can become first priority prior to even a first mortgage.

IRS liens can attach to a property and remain attached to the property even when the property transfers ownership. This is the reason why a lien search is always performed as part of your real estate closing.

Types of Liens

Water and Utility Bills (electric bill is not a lien)
Unpaid Property Taxes
Notice of Commencement
Open Permits
Code Enforcement Liens
Code Enforcement Violations
Judgments against all owners
Mechanic Liens
IRS and Federal Tax Liens

Please remember that the above liens may not show up in a title search. However, they may show up in a lien search. For this reason you should never decline ordering a lien search when you are closing on a real estate transaction.

Code Enforcement

The important thing to understand is that code enforcement liens normally attach not only to the property in question, but to all properties that the owner owns within the county where the property is located. If monies are owed to the city because of code enforcement violations, the city may lien all properties in that county until the owner rectifies the problem. For example if you are buying a short sale or foreclosure that is owned by an individual in Broward County and they have a code enforcement lien on one property then the code enforcement lien may attach to all of their other properties in that county. If the property you are buying has a code enforcement lien or violation then the owner will have to either clear the violation or have the buyer sign a hold harmless to the violation prior to closing. If the violation is minor, like a lawn that has not been mowed, then you may be able to get a credit from the bank and close and then rectify the situation yourself. Be on the look out for title companies that try and make you sign a hold harmless agreement making you ultimately responsible for the defect in title.

Closing Costs

- **Application Fee**: If there is a mortgage the lender (bank) can charge an application fee that can cost anywhere from $50 to $700
- **Underwriting Fees**: This is the fee that is charged by the lender that is approving you for a loan.

- **Flood Certificate Fee**: This fee is charged by the lender to determine if the property is in a FEMA flood hazard zone. If it is then an elevation certificate or proof of flood insurance will be required.
- **Tax Service Fee**: This is the fee that the lender charges to ensure that property taxes are paid on the property each year that the loan is in place.
- **Loan Origination Fee**: This is what the lender charges you as an upfront fee when they give you the loan.
- **Loan Discount Fee**: This is the fee that the lender charges for reducing the interest rate on the loan.
- **Document Preparation Fee**: The fee charged by the lender for preparing the loan documents.
- **Escrow Account**: Most lenders require you to escrow money in advance for property taxes and property insurance. This amount could be up to fourteen months of payments.
- **Prepaid Interest**: If your closing takes place between the first and the fifth day of the month, then you will receive a credit for the five days and your first payment will be due on the first day of the next month. If you close after the fifth day of the month, then you will be charged the remaining days of interest for the remainder of the month and your first payment will be due the first day of the following month (not next month).
- **Settlement Fee**: The closing cost charged by the title company or the attorney that is handling the closing.

- **Title Search**: This is the charge by the title company for performing the title search.
- **Title Insurance**: You have to have title insurance to close if there is a mortgage and a lender involved. Cash transactions do not require title insurance but you should always pay for a title insurance policy even if you are not required to have one. If you qualify for a reissue credit then the title insurance premium will be substantially reduced. It is typical in Broward or Miami-Dade Counties for the buyer to pay for title insurance and to choose the title agent. In the rest of the State of Florida it is customary for the seller to pay for title and to choose the title agent.
- **Intangible Taxes**: .0020% of loan amount charged by State of Florida at closing.
- **Document Stamps New Mortgage**: $0.35/ $100 for new money (borrowed money) such as a mortgage. This is a mandatory charge which is charged by the State of Florida.
- **Document Stamps Deed**: The seller is charged $0.70/ $100 on the sale price of the transaction. This is a mandatory charge which is charged by the State of Florida.
- **Recertification Fee**: This is the fee charged by the title company for reviewing the recorded deed and issuing the final title policy after the documents have been recorded. This essentially creates the effective date of the policy.

There can also be other fees such as postage, copy, notary, courier, etc. Many of these fees are negotiable and easily reduced. This is how your title company pads up your closing costs. Florida title insurance rates are governed by what is known as the promulgated rate which is the rate recommended by the state.

The **Promulgated Rate** for a title insurance policy in Florida is as follows:

- $5.75 per $1,000 of real estate value up to $100,000

- $5.00 per $1,000 of real estate value up to $1,000,000

How to read your HUD-1

Shortly before closing on a purchase or sale of any property, you will be given a Department of Housing and Urban Development Settlement Statement, also known as the HUD-1. This is your final account of all of the costs and figures related to the closing transaction (closing costs). Many of the costs listed in the HUD-1 form would also have been included in the Good Faith Estimate (GFE) of mortgage costs that you would have received from your lender. However, the HUD-1 amounts are final and the Good Faith Estimate is not. For this reason you should always review the HUD before you get to the closing table.

You may find some of the HUD-1 figures are different from those in your GFE. This could be because third-party fees such as appraisal fees ended up being slightly different than originally estimated. However, if there are large discrepancies, or new fees that were not in the GFE, check with your lender to see if there is a mistake that needs to be corrected. It is a good idea to get a copy of your final HUD-1 at least one day prior to closing in order to review it.

We will now take a closer look at the different sections of the HUD-1 form. In each section, there is one column showing the buyer's (or borrower's) figures and another column showing the seller's figures.

Sections A through I - General Information

The form starts with basic information about your loan. It includes such information as the type of loan, loan number, and settlement agent file number, location of the closing and the settlement date or date of closing. It also contains the buyer, seller and/or borrower's information as well as the property address.

(1) Section B - Type of Loan: There are several types of loan transactions. Examples include the following: FHA, RHS, Conventional Uninsured, VA or Conventional Insured.

(2) Section B – File Number: This is the Settlement Agent Company File Number.

(3) Section B – Loan Number: The lenders loan number.

(4) Section B – Mortgage Insurance Case Number: The Mortgage Insurance Case Number.

(5) Section C – Note: Disclosure.

(6) Section D: Name and Address of the Borrower.

(7) Section E: Name and Address of the Seller.

(8) Section F: Name and Address of the Lender.

(9) Section G: Property Address.

(10) Section H: Settlement Agent and Location of the Closing.

(11) Section I: Settlement Date or Closing Date.

(12) Section J - Summary of Borrower's Transaction: Section J shows the gross totals of the buyers costs, credits and the net amount the buyer will owe for the purchase. The total is listed by category:

(13) 100 - Gross Amount Due From Borrower: The amount the buyer owes, consisting of the property purchase price, the fees or settlement charges, items such as appliances purchased from the seller and payment of taxes the seller has prepaid (Line 120 is total).

(14) 200 - Amounts Paid By Or In Behalf of Borrower: The amounts the buyer has paid, such as the deposit, or financed, such as the mortgage financing or a mortgage the buyer is assuming. It also includes any sums the seller owes the buyer, such as unpaid taxes, utility costs or allowances for repairs (Line 220 is total).

(15) 300 - Cash at Settlement From/To Borrower: Carries the totals down to the bottom of the page. Line 301 is the same as Line 120. Line 302 is the same as Line 220. Line 303 is the total cash to/from the Buyer at closing.

(16) Section K - Summary of Seller's Transaction

Section K shows the gross totals of the sellers costs, credits and the net amount the seller will owe or receive for the sale. It lists the totals by category:

(17) 400 - Gross Amount Due to Seller: Reflects the credits due to the seller at closing, like the sales price of the home and/or any personal property that is being purchased by the buyers (Line 420 is total).

(18) 500 – Reductions in Amount Due to Seller: Reflects the charges or the debits of the seller. Examples include the settlement charges paid by the Seller (Line 502), payoffs of existing loans and proration's of items such as taxes and assessments to be credited to the buyer at closing (line 520 is total).

(19) 600 - Cash at Settlement From/To Seller: Carries the totals down to the bottom of the form. Line 601 is the same as line 420. Line 602 is the same as line 520. Line 603 is the cash due to/from Seller at closing.

(20) Section L (Settlement Charges)
Section L, on the second page of the form, shows all the specific costs for financing and processing of the transaction. It includes:

(21) 700. Total Sales/Broker's Commission based on price: The commission charged by the real estate broker.

(22) 800. Items Payable In Connection With Loan: The loan origination fee, any discount points paid to reduce the mortgage rate, the appraisal fee and credit report fee, the application fee for mortgage insurance, and the assumption fee, if you've assumed an existing mortgage. Fees that have been paid up front are marked P.O.C. (paid outside of closing) and will not be included in the total on Line 1400.

(23) 900. Items Required By Lender To Be Paid In Advance: The interest on the loan for the period before the first monthly payment, and the initial mortgage insurance and hazard or home insurance premiums (often covering the first year).

(24) 1000. Reserves Deposited With Lender: These are escrow items, which the lender holds to cover future expenses such as property taxes and annual assessments. In some cases, you may be asked to remit future hazard and mortgage premiums as escrow items. There is a maximum that can be charged.

(25) 1100. Title Charges: The costs of changing ownership of the property, such as the title services and cost of title insurance. If the fee is payable to a third party, such as the notary or attorney, it is indicated. If one agent performs more than one service, the fees may be lumped together on one line.

(26) 1200. Government Recording and Transfer Charges: City, county and state taxes or stamps needed to transfer ownership are listed here. The buyer often pays the deed and mortgage recording fees.

(27) 1300. Additional Settlement Charges: Items such as surveys, inspections for such things as pests and lead-based paint, and home warranties.

(28) 1400. Total Settlement Charges: The sum total of all of the above fees. The amount listed in the buyer's (or borrower's) column should be identical to the amount listed as "settlement charges to borrower" on page one, line 103, while the amount in the seller's column should be the same as the "settlement charges to seller" on page one, line 502.

It's important to read through the HUD-1 form carefully and determine that it's complete and accurate. You and the settlement agent will then both sign it to authorize payment of the funds. Once that's done, the home is yours.

OMB Approval No. 2502-0265

A. Settlement Statement (HUD-1)

B. Type of Loan

(1) 1. ☐ FHA 2. ☐ RHS 3. ☐ Conv. Unins. 4. ☐ VA 5. ☐ Conv. Ins.

6. File Number: **(2)** 7. Loan Number: **(3)** 8. Mortgage Insurance Case Number: **(4)**

(5) **C. Note:** This form is furnished to give you a statement of actual settlement costs. Amounts paid to and by the settlement agent are shown. Items marked "(p.o.c.)" were paid outside the closing; they are shown here for informational purposes and are not included in the totals.

D. Name & Address of Borrower: **(6)**	E. Name & Address of Seller: **(7)**	F. Name & Address of Lender: **(8)**
G. Property Location: **(9)**	H. Settlement Agent: **(10)** Place of Settlement:	I. Settlement Date: **(11)**

(12) **J. Summary of Borrower's Transaction**

(13) **100. Gross Amount Due from Borrower**
101. Contract sales price	
102. Personal property	
103. Settlement charges to borrower (line 1400)	
104.	
105.	

Adjustment for items paid by seller in advance
106. City/town taxes	to	
107. County taxes	to	
108. Assessments	to	
109.		
110.		
111.		
112.		

120. Gross Amount Due from Borrower

(14) **200. Amounts Paid by or in Behalf of Borrower**
201. Deposit or earnest money	
202. Principal amount of new loan(s)	
203. Existing loan(s) taken subject to	
204.	
205.	
206.	
207.	
208.	
209.	

Adjustments for items unpaid by seller
210. City/town taxes	to	
211. County taxes	to	
212. Assessments	to	
213.		
214.		
215.		
216.		
217.		
218.		
219.		

220. Total Paid by/for Seller

(15) **300. Cash at Settlement from/to Borrower**
301. Gross amount due from borrower (line 120)	
302. Less amounts paid by/for borrower (line 220)	( )
303. Cash ☐ From ☐ To Borrower	

(16) **K. Summary of Seller's Transaction**

(17) **400. Gross Amount Due to Seller**
401. Contract sales price	
402. Personal property	
403.	
404.	
405.	

Adjustments for items paid by seller in advance
406. City/town taxes	to	
407. County taxes	to	
408. Assessments	to	
409.		
410.		
411.		
412.		

420. Gross Amount Due to Seller

(18) **500. Reductions In Amount Due to Seller**
501. Excess deposit (see instructions)	
502. Settlement charges to seller (line 1400)	
503. Existing loan(s) taken subject to	
504. Payoff of first mortgage loan	
505. Payoff of second mortgage loan	
506.	
507.	
508.	
509.	

Adjustments for items unpaid by seller
510. City/town taxes	to	
511. County taxes	to	
512. Assessments	to	
513.		
514.		
515.		
516.		
517.		
518.		
519.		

520. Total Reduction Amount Due Seller

(19) **600. Cash at Settlement to/from Seller**
601. Gross amount due to seller (line 420)	
602. Less reductions in amount due seller (line 520)	( )
603. Cash ☐ To ☐ From Seller	

The Public Reporting Burden for this collection of information is estimated at 35 minutes per response for collecting, reviewing, and reporting the data. This agency may not collect this information, and you are not required to complete this form, unless it displays a currently valid OMB control number. No confidentiality is assured; this disclosure is mandatory. This is designed to provide the parties to a RESPA covered transaction with information during the settlement process.

Previous editions are obsolete   Page 1 of 3   HUD-1

		Paid From Borrower's Funds at Settlement	Paid From Seller's Funds at Settlement
(20)	**L. Settlement Charges**		
(21)	**700. Total Real Estate Broker Fees**		
	Division of commission (line 700) as follows:		
	701. $ to		
	702. $ to		
	703. Commission paid at settlement		
	704.		
(22)	**800. Items Payable in Connection with Loan**		
	801. Our origination charge $ (from GFE #1)		
	802. Your credit or charge (points) for the specific interest rate chosen $ (from GFE #2)		
	803. Your adjusted origination charges (from GFE A)		
	804. Appraisal fee to (from GFE #3)		
	805. Credit report to (from GFE #3)		
	806. Tax service to (from GFE #3)		
	807. Flood certification (from GFE #3)		
	808.		
(23)	**900. Items Required by Lender to Be Paid in Advance**		
	901. Daily interest charges from to @ $ /day (from GFE #10)		
	902. Mortgage insurance premium for months to (from GFE #3)		
	903. Homeowner's insurance for years to (from GFE #11)		
	904.		
(24)	**1000. Reserves Deposited with Lender**		
	1001. Initial deposit for your escrow account (from GFE #9)		
	1002. Homeowner's insurance months @ $ per month $		
	1003. Mortgage insurance months @ $ per month $		
	1004. Property taxes months @ $ per month $		
	1005. months @ $ per month $		
	1006. months @ $ per month $		
	1007. Aggregate Adjustment -$		
(25)	**1100. Title Charges**		
	1101. Title services and lender's title insurance (from GFE #4)		
	1102. Settlement or closing fee $		
	1103. Owner's title insurance (from GFE #5)		
	1104. Lender's title insurance $		
	1105. Lender's title policy limit $		
	1106. Owner's title policy limit $		
	1107. Agent's portion of the total title insurance premium $		
	1108. Underwriter's portion of the total title insurance premium $		
(26)	**1200. Government Recording and Transfer Charges**		
	1201. Government recording charges (from GFE #7)		
	1202. Deed $ Mortgage $ Releases $		
	1203. Transfer taxes (from GFE #8)		
	1204. City/County tax/stamps Deed $ Mortgage $		
	1205. State tax/stamps Deed $ Mortgage $		
	1206.		
(27)	**1300. Additional Settlement Charges**		
	1301. Required services that you can shop for (from GFE #6)		
	1302. $		
	1303. $		
	1304.		
	1305.		
(28)	**1400. Total Settlement Charges (enter on lines 103, Section J and 502, Section K)**		

24

Comparison of Good Faith Estimate (GFE) and HUD-1 Charges		Good Faith Estimate	HUD-1
Charges That Cannot Increase	**HUD-1 Line Number**		
Our origination charge	# 801		
Your credit or charge (points) for the specific interest rate chosen	# 802		
Your adjusted origination charges	# 803		
Transfer taxes	#1203		

Charges That in Total Cannot Increase More Than 10%		Good Faith Estimate	HUD-1
Government recording charges	# 1201		
	#		
	#		
	#		
	#		
	#		
	#		
	#		
Total			
Increase between GFE and HUD-1 Charges		$ or	%

Charges That Can Change		Good Faith Estimate	HUD-1
Initial deposit for your escrow account	#1001		
Daily interest charges	# 901 $ /day		
Homeowner's insurance	# 903		
	#		
	#		
	#		

Loan Terms

Your initial loan amount is	$
Your loan term is	▨▨▨ years
Your initial interest rate is	▨▨▨ %
Your initial monthly amount owed for principal, interest, and any mortgage insurance is	$ ▨▨▨▨▨ includes ☐ Principal ☐ Interest ☐ Mortgage Insurance
Can your interest rate rise?	☐ No. ☐ Yes, it can rise to a maximum of ▨▨%. The first change will be on ▨▨▨▨ and can change again every ▨▨▨ after ▨▨▨▨ . Every change date, your interest rate can increase or decrease by ▨▨%. Over the life of the loan, your interest rate is guaranteed to never be lower than ▨▨ % or higher than ▨▨ %.
Even if you make payments on time, can your loan balance rise?	☐ No. ☐ Yes, it can rise to a maximum of $ ▨▨▨▨ .
Even if you make payments on time, can your monthly amount owed for principal, interest, and mortgage insurance rise?	☐ No. ☐ Yes, the first increase can be on ▨▨▨ and the monthly amount owed can rise to $ ▨▨▨ . The maximum it can ever rise to is $ ▨▨▨ .
Does your loan have a prepayment penalty?	☐ No. ☐ Yes, your maximum prepayment penalty is $ ▨▨▨ .
Does your loan have a balloon payment?	☐ No. ☐ Yes, you have a balloon payment of $ ▨▨▨ due in ▨▨ years on ▨▨▨ .
Total monthly amount owed including escrow account payments	☐ You do not have a monthly escrow payment for items, such as property taxes and homeowner's insurance. You must pay these items directly yourself. ☐ You have an additional monthly escrow payment of $ ▨▨▨ that results in a total initial monthly amount owed of $ ▨▨▨ . This includes principal, interest, any mortgage insurance and any items checked below: ☐ Property taxes ☐ Homeowner's insurance ☐ Flood insurance ☐ ▨▨▨ ☐ ▨▨▨ ☐ ▨▨▨

Note: If you have any questions about the Settlement Charges and Loan Terms listed on this form, please contact your lender.

Deeds

A deed is the document that transfers ownership of real estate. It contains the names of the old and new owners, a legal description or land description, the parcel identification number of the property and is signed by the person transferring the property. A deed does not necessarily indicate a sale.

You should always have a deed when transferring property. You cannot sell, transfer or convey real estate without having something in writing. This written instrument is known as a deed and it should be recorded in the public records at the courthouse in the same county as where the property is located.

The deed should describe the property being sold, conveyed, or transferred, the names of the current owner(s), and the new owner(s), including marital status of all parties. One of the most common defects that we find is where only one party has signed the deed without including their marital status. If they are married, then the joiner of spouse or non homestead language is required. Primary residences are required to have permission of the spouse to sell the property. Investment properties of married individuals may be sold without the spouse's consent or signature (provided they were not on the deed originally) and as long as the property is not their homestead. In addition to this, there will need to be non homestead language included on the deed.

Types of Deeds

Quit Claim Deed

A quit claim deed transfers the ownership interest the person has in the property. It is important to understand that if the person signing the quit claim has no ownership interest in the property then the quit claim deed is worthless. I can quit claim the Brooklyn Bridge to you. However, since I don't have any ownership in the Brooklyn Bridge the quit claim deed is worthless. For this reason you should never transfer property with a quit claim unless it is an intra family transfer and you know the owner. Quit claim deeds are often used in the case of divorce or transfer or a property between siblings or from parents to their children.

Grant Deed

A Grant Deed transfers your ownership interest and makes certain guarantees that the title hasn't already been transferred to someone else or been encumbered, except as describe in the grant deed. Most states use a Grant Deed which is substantially better than a quit claim deed.

Warranty Deed

A warranty deed transfers your ownership interest in the property and explicitly promises and guarantees, to the buyer, that you have good and clear marketable title to the property. A warranty deed may also promise to cure certain defects. This is the most common deed in the State of Florida.

Special Warranty Deed

A special warranty deed is the most common methods that a bank uses to transfer title to a bank owned property also known as an REO. The special warranty deed is a deed in which the seller conveys title to the buyer and agrees to protect the buyer against title defects or claims asserted by the bank or any other people who feel that they have a right to assert a claim against the property. With a special warranty deed the seller guarantees to the buyer that they have not done anything during the time that they held title to the property to impair the title in any way. For purposes of purchasing bank owned properties a special warranty deed is usually fine.

A deed should always be signed by the person who is transferring or selling the property. The deeds should be signed and notarized in front of a notary public, who will then sign and stamp it. All title companies have notaries in order to facilitate this process. The notarization means that a notary public has verified that the signature on the deed is a real signature. The signature must be notarized before the deed can be recorded.

In the State of Florida, executed deeds need to contain a notary signature and 2 witnesses per signature. One of the witnesses can be the notary, but they must sign in both spots. If there are two parties signing the deed, that are both in the same place at the same time, then the witness may sign for both parties. In the case of two parties that are signing at two different times and two different locations (not together) there will need to be four signature lines for the witnesses and two notary signatures. Remember that if you did not witness the signature you should not be signing the documents.

The deed should be recorded (made a part of public record) in the land records office or county clerks office in the county where the property is located. This office goes by different names in different states. In Florida it is usually the Clerk of Court which is at the county court house. For example in Palm Beach County it is called the Palm Beach County Clerk of Court.

Recording Fees

Recording fees in the State of Florida are $10.00 for the first page and $8.50 for each additional page. In some counties such as Palm Beach County they charge an extra $0.60 for indexing a legal description. These fees include documents that include up to four names. If there are more than four names, then each additional name is an additional dollar.

Recording a deed is very straight forward. You should take the signed, original deed to the county clerk at the court house. The clerk will take the deed, stamp it with the date, image a copy and give the original back to you. The first page of the document will consist of the date and time of recording, the official record book and page (where you can locate a copy of the deed), and a document control number. Copies of deeds are now located online in many counties.

Trust Deed (Deed of Trust)

A trust deed is also know as a deed of trust and is not the same as other types of deeds. A trust deed is not used to transfer property but is really just another term for a mortgage in states that are deed of trust states (see list below). Georgia calls their trust deed a Security Deed. Connecticut calls theirs a Mortgage Deed.

A trust deed transfers the title to a "trustee," which is often a trust or a title company, which holds the land as security for a loan. When the loan is paid off, title is transferred to the borrower. It works very much the same as the way car companies hold the title to a vehicle until you have paid off your note on the car. The trustee has no powers to convey or transfer the property unless the borrower defaults on the loan. If the borrower defaults, then the trustee can sell the property and pay the lender back from the proceeds, without first going to court. This occurs only in states where a deed of trust is used. Florida uses a mortgage and not a deed of trust so you actually own title to your property in Florida from the date of purchase.

Here is a list of states and whether they are a Mortgage or Deed of Trust State:

AL Alabama Mortgage
AK Alaska Deed of Trust
AZ Arizona Deed of Trust
AR Arkansas Mortgage
CA California Deed of Trust
CO Colorado Deed of Trust
CT Connecticut Mortgage Deed
DE Delaware Mortgage
DC DC Columbia Deed of Trust

MT Montana Deed of Trust
NE Nebraska Deed of Trust
NV Nevada Deed of Trust
NH New Hampshire Mortgage
NJ New Jersey Mortgage
NM New Mexico Deed of Trust
NY New York Mortgage
NC North Carolina Deed of Trust
ND North Dakota Mortgage

FL Florida Mortgage
GA Georgia Security Deed
HI Hawaii Mortgage
ID Idaho Deed of Trust
IL Illinois Mortgage
IN Indiana Mortgage
IA Iowa Mortgage
KS Kansas Mortgage
KY Kentucky Mortgage
LA Louisiana Mortgage
ME Maine Mortgage
MD Maryland Deed of Trust
MA Massachusetts Mortgage
MI Michigan Mortgage
MN Minnesota Mortgage
MS Mississippi Deed of Trust
MO Missouri Deed of Trust

OH Ohio Mortgage
OK Oklahoma Mortgage
OR Oregon Deed of Trust
PA Pennsylvania Mortgage
RI Rhode Island Mortgage
SC South Carolina Mortgage
SD South Dakota Mortgage
TN Tennessee Deed of Trust
TX Texas Deed of Trust
UT Utah Deed of Trust
VT Vermont Mortgage
VA Virginia Deed of Trust
VI Virgin Islands Mortgage
WA Washington Deed of Trust
WV West Virginia Deed of Trust
WI Wisconsin Mortgage
WY Wyoming Mortgage

Should You Use Your Title Company or the Banks Title Company?

In Florida, it is customary for the seller to pay for the title policy and to pick the title agent. The exceptions are Broward and Miami-Dade Counties where it is customary for the buyer to pay for the title policy and to pick the title agent. In Palm Beach County and the rest of the State Of Florida it is customary for the seller to pay. Usually whoever picks the title agent also pays for the title policy.

If you are buying bank owned properties then you should be especially cautious. If you are using the bank's title company then this means that the title company has a relationship with the seller and not with you. There have been several cases where our investors have used the banks title company and had serious title defects and issues.

The title companies that represent the bank are typically known as "title mills" which means that they are closing hundreds of transactions per month for a bank. This means that the bank is effectively the title company's biggest and best client and so the title company is much more concerned with the relationship with the bank than with you. Another issue is that because they are processing so many files, they make many mistakes which your title company, that represents you, may not make.

One example of an issue that we have seen is where there was open code enforcement violations secured against a property that was going to cost a buyer over $5,000 to remedy. It was the banks title companies' procedure to have the buyer sign a "hold harmless agreement" which effectively means that the banks title company is willing to close the transaction with a title defect and make it the buyer's problem. This is a classic example of why you don't want to let the bank choose the title company even if it saves you money. You are better off paying for your own title policy and choosing your own title company that will have your best interests at heart.

Another issue if you plan on simultaneous or double closing a transaction with the banks title company will be that the banks title company will simply disallow you from going through with the simultaneous or double closing. Many title companies that represent the banks are unfamiliar with these types of closings and how the procedure works. If you are planning on a simultaneous or double closing on the property with an end buyer then using the banks title company could effectively prevent your transaction from closing which would eliminate your profit. This is yet another reason why you want to choose your title company.

Lastly, if you plan on closing an REO transaction time is of the essence. It is important the title company will record the deed as soon as possible. This becomes an issue when you are planning to resell to an FHA buyer and there are title seasoning requirements. We have seen several cases where the banks title company holds on to a batch of deeds and waits as long as thirty days to record these deeds.

If you have a relationship with a title company they should use a courier to immediately deliver the document to the courthouse for recording. If you are simultaneous or double closing then it is imperative that the deeds are recorded in the correct sequence preventing a chain of title defect. This is yet another example of why you should always choose your own title company.

Transactional Funding

If you have a signed contract and are wholesaling your transaction to an end buyer, then if you do not have the funds to fund the first transaction you will need transactional funding. Transactional funding is perfect for bank owned properties and short sales that you are selling to an end buyer. Since banks do not allow assignable contracts you are going to need to schedule a simultaneous or double closing with your end buyer. Double closings also known as simultaneous closings allow you to schedule two back to back closings for the same property on the same day. You will need to have a source of funds to pay for the first transaction. This is where transactional funding (also known as same day funds) is needed.

If you are a private mentoring student with the Distressed Real Estate Institute and you have a closing that needs transactional funding then we may be able to fund your transaction. However, in order for us to fund your transaction we need to review it and make sure that it meets the following criteria:

You must use our approved title company or attorney for your closing

How does transactional funding work?

If you are looking to simultaneously close a bank owned property then you will have two contracts and two closings. The first contract is between the bank (seller) and you (buyer). The second contract is between you (seller) and your end buyer (buyer). The end buyer is the person that will ultimately be the long term owner of the property.

Example of transactional funding for a simultaneous or double closing:

A – Bank
B – You
C – End Buyer

You have a contract with the bank to purchase a bank owned property at $40,000 (first contract). This is known as the A-B transaction.

You market this property to your cash buyers and you find a buyer at $50,000. You sign a contract with this buyer (you being the seller) and them being the buyer (second contract). This is known as the B-C transaction.

The difference between the two contracts (after deducting closing costs) is your profit which you will walk away with at the closing. We recommend that your contract with your end buyer contain a clause stating that the end buyer will pay all closing and acquisition costs. This is important because you want to ensure that you have a net profit number that will not be substantially reduced by the double closing costs. You should always pass these costs on to the end buyer when wholesaling a property (if you can).

Double Closings

Since there are two contracts there are two closings. This means you will pay double closing costs. There are ways to avoid paying double closing costs like using an entity such as a Land Trust or an LLC. There are advantages and disadvantages to using these methods. We advise you to consult with your attorney or CPA for advice on the type of entity and its merits. Also please note that land trusts that are common in Florida might not be legal or common in other states.

What are the fees for transactional funding?

The transactional funding fee is 2% of the funded amount plus a $495 processing fee. There is a minimum transactional funding fee of $1,250. For example if you were to request funding in the amount of $40,000 your fee would be $800 + $495 = $1,295.

What if the bank insists on using their title company?

We will only provide transactional funding if you use our approved title company or attorney for your closing.

What do I do if I find an end buyer?

You should always take a deposit from your end buyer that is at least twice the amount of your initial deposit and you should always only accept cleared funds like a cashiers check or wire transfer directly to the title company or attorney. It is your responsibility to provide both contracts to the title company or attorney and to clearly label all cashiers checks and wires with the property address. It is also your responsibility to communicate with the Distressed Real Estate Institute about the transaction.

Can you help me find an end buyer?

Yes, if we find a buyer for your transaction then we will split the profit with you 50/50. If we are providing transactional funding you will still be responsible for paying the transactional funding fee. Many of our buyers are looking for rental properties and first time home buyer properties that are valued at less than $75,000. The highest demand for housing exists at the lower price points of the market since there are first time home buyers and investors looking to buy these properties. We have many cash buyers for these types of properties in South Florida.

Where Do We Provide Transactional Funding?

We will provide transactional funding for properties that are located anywhere in Florida. Please keep in mind that transactional funding is only offered to individuals where we have a partnership or beneficial interest in the property. Since we are not mortgage brokers or lenders we cannot offer transactional funding for any transaction where we do not have a beneficial interest in the transaction.

Our investors purchase and wholesale properties in Miami-Dade County, Broward County, Palm Beach County and St Lucie County. Since we are based in Fort Lauderdale, we prefer properties that are within 90 minutes driving distance. Each property needs to be inspected by an approved inspector from the Distressed Real Estate Institute before we can provide transactional funding.

There is an upfront $150 fee to inspect the property which is credited back to you if we provide the funding. This fee will be credited back to you at closing on your HUD-1. Most of the transactions that we fund are within a 150 mile radius of Fort Lauderdale which typically covers anything between Miami and Port St Lucie, FL. We will fund transactions in other parts of Florida but we might charge a higher inspection fee.

How does the Distressed Real Estate Institute's Private Mentoring Program Work?

The Private Mentoring Program is a program that the Distressed Real Estate Institute offers to students that are looking for individual one to one private training.

The Private Mentoring Program involves 32 hours of training with a Private Mentoring Coach and also includes access to the Distressed Real Estate Boot Camp and the Home Study Course. For more information please visit the following link to learn more about the private mentoring program offered by the Distressed Real Estate Institute.

www.lexlevinrad.com/mentoring.html

Do you need transactional funding for your transaction?

First speak to the Distressed Real Estate Institute by calling 800-617-2884 to make sure that we are willing to provide transactional funding for your transaction. If you do not have both contracts with one of our approved title companies or attorneys **then we will not fund your transaction**. There are no exceptions to this since it is too risky for us to wire our money to title companies that we do not have a relationship with. If you meet all of the above requirements then please submit the following:

- Purchase and sale contract between the bank (seller) and you as the buyer. (A to B)
- Purchase and sale contract between you (as the seller) and the end buyer who will be the ultimate owner of the property. (B to C)
- Proof of funds letter for the end buyer showing that they have the cash to close or a hard money loan in place.
- Deposit in escrow for both contracts (cashiers check or wire transfer only).

PLEASE NOTE THAT THE BUYER ON THE FIRST TRANSACTION MUST BE THE SAME NAME AS THE SELLER ON THE SECOND TRANSACTION

Please fax all documents to 561-948-0410 or scan and email to:

Lex@LexLevinrad.com or Kevin@KevinTacher.com

If you have any questions about transactional funding, simultaneous or double closings or wholesaling your transaction please call Lex Levinrad at 800-617-2884 ext 1 or call Kevin Tacher at 954-335-9305 ext 102.

Attorney vs. Title Company

One of the most common questions that I am asked is whether to use a title company or an attorney for the closing. There are advantages to both and obviously I would prefer that you do your closing with us at Independence Title.

Attorneys know the law much more than a title company would. For that reason they usually charge more money. Typically a closing at a law firm will cost quite a bit more than a closing at a title company. Since attorneys bill by the hour, their time is very valuable and using their time will cost you for your closing. However, there could be some benefits if for example the attorney is your attorney and you are utilizing the attorney's other services for example preparing a mortgage.

The disadvantage of using an attorney for your closing is that attorneys are not monitored as closely by the state. The Florida Bar already monitors attorneys and presumably the attorney knows the law of what he/she can and cannot do in regards to escrow accounts etc.

Title companies have much stricter requirements with their underwriters. Typically an underwriter will require monthly reconciliation from a title company to verify escrow deposits and accounts whereas attorneys do not necessarily have this requirement.

It is hard to generalize, but generally speaking attorneys are more expensive. Some attorneys work for the banks and REO companies and for this reason there may be a conflict of interest. You should always have someone reviewing your title commitment and lien search that is not affiliated with the seller or working on behalf of the seller.

Most real estate companies in Florida have a financial connection to a title company. They suggest or encourage their agents to refer their clients to a specific title company for the simple fact that the real estate company makes an additional fee from the settlement on the property. Always be careful when choosing your title company. Ask the title company if they have any affiliations with the real estate agent, mortgage broker, lender or seller in order to ensure that there is no conflict of interest.

The Real Estate Settlement Procedures Act

The Real Estate Settlement Procedures Act of 1974 (RESPA) was established to protect individuals by making real estate settlements more transparent. RESPA also establishes guidelines in order to control abusive practices like excessive junk fees that make closings more expensive than they should be. When there is a mortgage and a lender involved, RESPA controls the regulations related to the closing

New Regulations for RESPA

The Department of Housing and Urban Development (HUD) is responsible for establishing the RESPA laws that cover closings of residential real estate transactions. The newly updated regulations (regulation X) regulate all types of residential real estate closings. These laws regulate all title companies, attorneys, title examiners, mortgage companies, insurance companies, appraisers, real estate agents, inspectors, and underwriters. The purpose of the new RESPA regulations was to make title insurance, and real estate closings easier to understand and more transparent to the consumer allowing the consumer to shop for the lowest rates.

Impact on Florida Real Estate Closings

In most counties in Florida, the standard procedure is for the seller to select the closing agent and for the seller to pay for title insurance. The standard real estate sale contract form currently in use, as provided by the Florida Association of Realtors (FAR) and the Florida Bar (BAR) is called the FAR/BAR contract which is widely used by most real estate agents. This FAR/BAR contract allows for either the buyer or the seller to pay for title insurance. Usually the individual completing the form (real estate agent) will use standard procedures, but it is important for the buyer to understand that they can be made responsible for paying for title insurance.

The FAR/BAR contract also allows either the purchaser or the seller to select the title company. We always recommend that you choose your own title company, even if you have to pay for the title insurance premium.

This way you can ensure that the title company is looking out for your best interest as the buyer and not the seller's interests. This is especially important with bank owned REO properties since the title company receives so much business from the bank and the contract is very skewed in favor of the bank. It is prudent for you to use a title company or attorney to review the contract before you sign it. This is yet another reason why you should use your own title company.

The new law effective January 1st, 2010 will make it much easier for buyers to select their own title company.

7 Title Insurance Tips and Secrets

Secret # 1 - Simultaneous Policies

If you buy a house and get an owner's policy for $100,000 and you obtain financing to buy the house the lender will require their own title insurance policy. This policy is called a simultaneous policy which means that you pay full price for the owner's policy and you get the simultaneous policy for a promulgated rate cost of only $25. Many title companies increase the cost from $25 to $250 or more. Knowing this tip can save you hundreds of dollars at every closing.

Secret # 2 - Promulgated Rate

Title insurance promulgated rates are the lowest title insurance premium a title company is allowed to charge. That is, the state sets a minimum rate and title companies have to charge a rate that is the same or higher than this promulgated rate. It would benefit you, the consumer, to know what the states promulgated rate is in order to see how much you are being charged over the minimum rate. Know what the promulgated rate is in your state and don't pay more than this minimum rate. As a title company, we believe that charging more than this rate is not justified for our clients. Unfortunately not all settlement agents feel the same way. Closing costs vary substantially. That is why the new RESPA laws were established in order to make the market more competitive and fair for the consumer.

Secret # 3 – Escrow Agreements and Deposits

You should always use an escrow agreement which stipulates in the event of a default by one party (buyer or seller), what the procedure and instructions are for the title company or attorney and how they should manage the escrow deposit and release of the escrow deposit.

When you receive proof of deposit for your buyers (if you are a seller), you want to make sure that the title company has received cleared good funds into their escrow account. For this reason, you should make sure that all deposits are in cleared funds only. Never accept personal checks if you do not know the buyer and that their funds will clear. A stop payment can be issued on cashier's checks or printed fraudulently. Always insist on a wire transfer of funds in order to ensure that the deposits are cleared funds. The same applies to the funds required for closing. Always use wire transfers if you want to be safe.

Secret # 4 - Reissue Rate Credit

If the seller can produce to the buyer, a title policy that was issued in the past three years, then the title company can provide a reissue rate that can be as much as a 40% discount on the new title insurance policy. Always ask the seller if they have a copy of their original title insurance policy if the property was purchased by them in the previous three years. You can receive this reissue rate credit for your new owners' title policy. The actual amount of the credit is the same amount regardless of whether the policy is one, two or three years old. If the policy is older than three years then you will not be able to receive the reissue rate credit.

In the case of a refinance, you can get a reissue credit if you can provide a copy of your title policy regardless of when you purchased the property. It is imperative that you store your title policy in a safe and secure place such as a safe.

Secret # 5 – Can you prepare your own Deed

A common issue that we see when it comes to title examination is the use of deeds that are purchased at the local store. While these deeds are valid and can be used, you need to keep a few important things in mind. When you first purchase a property you are taking legal title. Why would you jeopardize your equitable interest in the property by preparing a fill in the blank document from the local store? There are many title companies and or attorneys that would prepare a deed for a minimal expense to you as the consumer. This is especially true if you have an existing relationship with them. Should you decide to prepare one of these yourself, please keep a few items in mind. All deeds should include the name of the grantor (seller) and grantee (buyer). Deeds should include the marital status of all parties involved. The complete legal description and parcel identification number should be included in the deed. Please do not copy the legal description from the county property appraiser's office website as this is usually an abbreviated version. Finally make sure the deed contains a signature of the grantor (seller), two witnesses and a notary. Please see the section on deeds to learn more.

Secret # 6 – Controlled Business Arrangements

A Controlled Business Arrangement is where a bank, real estate broker, real estate agent, mortgage broker, or title company may have an agreement with each other to provide their services to their clients for a referral fee in return. While this is not illegal or necessarily unethical, you always want to ask the question "Do you have a controlled business arrangement with anyone involved in this real estate transaction?". This is especially important with real estate because you want to make sure that your best interest is being protected. Unfortunately, some individuals are more concerned about getting their referral fee as opposed to representing their client's best interests. Please note that it is a violation of Florida Bar regulations for an attorney to pay a referral fee to any person other than another attorney.

Secret # 7 – Do you Interview your Title Company?

Do you interview your Title Company before you choose them to handle your business? If not then you should try and ask these questions the next time you have a real estate closing.

- Ask them if they are experts in their field, or if they are just a "middleman" company that refers their business out to another firm to actually issue your policy.

- Take a look at the company's name or website address for a clue if they are a real company. There is so much fraud you want to make sure you are dealing with a reputable company.

- Do they have a database of satisfied, well-known customers, or just a list of anonymous "testimonials" that could have been written by anyone? Ask them to supply you with verifiable references. If they can't, chances are they don't want you to find out something you shouldn't. I would suggest calling at least two of their customers to verify the company's integrity.

- Will they actually follow through on your transaction, or just skip town leaving you to start at the beginning? Are they ethical and do they implement world class business practices? Do they have an actual phone number that dials through to a live person or a virtual assistant?

Title Insurance Fraud

It is very important to know your title company and have a good working relationship with them. It is also a good idea to know who the principals of the company are since you are depositing your escrow funds with this company and you want to minimize the risk of Title Insurance Fraud.

The most common type of fraud is where the title company or attorney "dips" into the escrow account in order to cover short falls. Any principal of an escrow account can withdraw funds from that account so it can be very tempting for someone with a criminal mind. Even legitimate individuals with no criminal intent can get in over their head by borrowing from their escrow account to make payroll or pay rent. If they are a little short for the month it can be very tempting to dip into the escrow account and then pay back the escrow account from future anticipated fees. The problem lies with the fact that once they make a habit of doing this it can get out of hand. Before you know it, they are borrowing from their escrow account and cannot repay the money. At that point they start using new escrow deposits to pay off the old ones and now you have a classic case of a Ponzi scheme. This is fraud plain and simple and will ultimately put the principal in jail.

Unfortunately this has happened a lot lately. Here are some examples from recent headlines. These stories were taken from www.mortgagefraudblog.com which is a very interesting read.

Weed and Associates Title Company

In Florida, a title agent accused of stealing more than $1.1 million in customer escrow funds took the money and went on a Las Vegas gambling spree along with her boyfriend and coworkers. Kathryn Knight, 37, also known as Kathryn Weed, was operating Weed & Associates Title Services when American Pioneer Title Insurance Company conducted an audit and discovered discrepancies in Weed & Associates escrow account.

Fraud detectives determined that Knight misappropriated in excess of $1.1 million from the escrow account and used these funds to buy vehicles, the Las Vegas getaway and make a down payment on a $9 million land purchase. Her title agent license was immediately revoked and she faces up to 60 years in prison if convicted on the charges, according to Florida's Division of Insurance Fraud.

Attorney Scott Alan Salomon

Scott Alan Salomon, a title and closing attorney and owner of Platinum Title Services Corp., Coral Springs, Florida, surrendered to Broward County authorities on charges of issuing a forged instrument, two counts of grand theft, mortgage fraud and misappropriating monies. The felony charges against Salomon arise from allegations that he failed to satisfy prior mortgages in at least two refinance closings and failed to place title insurance.

At least one consumer lost a home as a result when the attorney failed to pay off her prior mortgage and didn't inform her that his title insurance agency appointment had been cancelled by the Attorneys Title Insurance Fund. According to officials, Salomon is also alleged to have used forged closing letters in at least two refinances. His agency license has already been revoked.

Flagler Title Company

Roger C. Gamblin, 61, and Peggy L. Gamblin, 53, both of Royal Palm Beach, Florida, have been indicted by a federal grand jury sitting in West Palm Beach, Florida, for allegedly defrauded companies and individuals out of approximately $10 million between July 2005 and May 2008.

According to the indictment, the husband and wife owners and operators of Flagler Title Company teamed up to steal money from the escrow account for Flagler Title Company to cover company operating expenses and personal expenses. The fraud was committed by promising the Title Insurance Companies they represented and various companies and individuals with outstanding real estate transactions that money in the Flagler Title Company escrow accounts would be used solely in connection with real estate transactions and their fees would not be disbursed until the transactions occurred and Flagler had earned their fee. Instead, the Gamblins caused money to be transferred without completing the transactions or obtaining permission from the title insurers, buyers, sellers and mortgagees involved in the property transactions.

J & E Universal Title Services

Evelyn Marrero and Jorge Bacallao, husband and wife, both of Miami, Florida, were sentenced to 8 years and 4 years of imprisonment, respectively, to be followed by terms of supervised release.

Marrero and Bacallao, the owners of the now-defunct J & E Universal Title Services, Inc. pled guilty in December 2008 to conspiracy and wire fraud charges, in violation of 18 U.S.C. §§ 1349 and 1343, arising out of a multi-million dollar mortgage fraud scheme. They were charged in a multi-count indictment along with co-defendants Aivet Loarca, Marilyn De La Paz (a/k/a/ "Marilyn Martis"), Daisy Gonzalez, Loaisa Rodriguez, and Elena Garman.

According to the Indictment and evidence presented in court, Marrero and Bacallao owned and operated, along with De La Paz, J & E Universal Title Services in Miami-Dade County, Florida. Marrero, Bacallao, and De La Paz participated in fraudulent purchase and sale transactions of residential property as the title and closing agent through J & E Universal.

In order to carry out the scheme, Marrero, Bacallao, and De La Paz conspired with Loarca and Gonzalez, who worked as mortgage loan brokers, to submit fraudulent applications for mortgage loans. The applications included materially false information about the borrowers' employment verification, income and deposit funds verification, and rent verification. As part of the transactions, the defendants used "straw" purchasers, including Rodriguez, or otherwise used stolen identities, which Garman helped obtain.

Following the lending institutions' approval of the applications, the institutions wire-transferred the loan proceeds to the defendants' title company for closing. The defendants regularly used J & E Universal as the title closing agent. Through J & E Universal, the defendants used the loan proceeds to pay creditors, themselves, and other co-conspirators.

In sum, from early 2005 through late 2007, the defendants participated in some or all of more than 30 real estate transactions in Miami-Dade County with funded loans totaling almost $13 million.

Judge Jordan has sentenced four of the defendants in this case, including Rodriguez, who received 24 months' imprisonment on May 12th; Gonzalez, who received 30 months' imprisonment on May 26th; De La Paz, who received 96 months' imprisonment on May 28th; and Loarca, who received 72 months' imprisonment on June 2nd.

The moral of the story is this. Know your title company and know who you are dealing with. Don't use the banks title company. Establish a relationship with a title company whose principals are individuals that you trust and have a relationship with. This will build good will and trust in your relationship and you will be able to negotiate better closing costs for future transactions.

Summary

We hope you enjoyed reading Title Insurance Tips and Secrets as much as we have enjoyed writing it. If you can only remember a few things from this book please remember the following important items:

- Always get a title insurance policy for all transactions even for simultaneous or double closings.
- Choose your own title company
- Review the title commitment.
- Ask about any requirements on Schedule B-I.
- Review the lien search.
- Ask questions if you do not understand something throughout your closing process.
- Do not sign your closing documents until you have reviewed all of the above.

Please join us at the local real estate meetings that we host and attend in South Florida. We have local meetings in South Florida on the first Tuesday and Thursday of each month and you can usually find us at all of the local real estate events. We love investing in real estate and we really enjoy speaking with real estate investors so please make sure to introduce yourself.

If you enjoyed reading this book and would like to share your positive feedbacks and thoughts about this book we will be very happy to post your positive testimonials on our website.

We hope that you choose Independence Title for your next closing. However, if you don't we hope that you learned something useful from this book that will help you save some money. Finally, remember to watch out for potential problems at your next closing.

To your success as a real estate investor, real estate professional or consumer.

Kevin

Kevin S. Tacher
CEO, Independence Title
www.MyTitleCo.com
www.KevinTacher.com
www.TitleTuesdays.com
www.MotivationalMondays.net

Lex

Lex Levinrad
Founder, Distressed Real Estate Institute
www.LexLevinrad.com

Testimonials

"No one understands title insurance better than Kevin Tacher and Lex Levinrad. Having vast experience in the industry and being highly skilled at utilizing trusted, professional networks, they have been offering added-value to their clients for years. This book reveals the pertinent facts and insights which will help consumers and industry professionals alike make informed, strategic decisions for optimum results; it is a definite must read."

Ivan Misner, NY Times Bestselling Author and Founder of BNI and Referral Institute

"In this book, Kevin does what he always does, and that is, add extreme value to everyone; regardless of whether that person does business with him or not. However, knowing him as I do, I suspect that if you do work with him, you'll be glad you did."

Bob Burg, National Bestselling Author and Co-Author of *The Go-Giver* and *Go-Givers Sell More*

Once again Kevin has put himself out there to help others. Reading his book you can see how much he cares about his work and cares even more about the people he works with.

Mike Macedonio, Co-Author of New York Times Best Seller, "Truth or Delusion, Busting Networking's Biggest Myths"

<u>Testimonials</u>

"Anyone and everyone investing in real estate along with all real estate professionals must read this comprehensive overview on title insurance. The tips will save you money and minimize headaches. Kevin and Lex's commitment to integrity and service is evident in the way they conduct business and in their dissemination of information in this book."

David Dweck, Investor, Realtor, President Boca Real Estate Investment Club

When I started working with Kevin he asked me "Are you sure you can handle all the new business that will come your way?" I questioned him when he made that comment, but he was right! I now have two full time staff assistants, 647 real estate professionals and am working on positioning myself to effectively manage my business at this new level. Kevin's coaching and support for my agent's success is like no other. His sincere interest begins with elevating other people's success before his own. This book shares another reason why Kevin adds value to everyone in his circle of influence.

Cynthia L. Benchick, Realtor & Broker/Owner Charles Rutenberg Realty, LLC

<u>Notes</u>

<u>Notes</u>

<u>Notes</u>

Notes